V. ⸺

Volume One:
Lessons Learned in the War For My Heart

By:
Chris Faenza

aka
Fucking Metal Chris
@wordsonfxckingpaper
On Instagram

First Edition
KDP 2020

I refuse to fill a book with generic inspirational words and positive advice and tell you that it's poetry. That is not why I am here, nor am I here to repeat the motivational lying bullshit you want to hear. My goal is to tell truths so honest that you will have no choice but to look inside yourself and re-evaluate the way you look at love and loss and pain and hope and life.

That isn't to say that some of the things I have to say won't sound cliche. Sometimes reality is just that way. These cliches exist for a reason, after all. I don't want to run from them, but I don't ever want to rely on them or find myself believing that things have to be the way they are.

Sometimes everything has to change.

We all reach a point where we realize that the status quo in our life is not good enough anymore. Take my hand and together we can walk through that door.

I don't write fiction
I write GOSPEL
And the honesty
Leaves you *weak*

This is not poetry
It's brutal honesty
My story laid bare
For the world to see

The truth in these words
Has toppled Gods
And given birth to worlds
That wouldn't exist
There is meaning
In. Every. Fucking. Syllable. Of. This.

I write it down
I spit it out
These pages catch
What's left of my heart
Splattering on the paper
And I long to call it art

My words will linger
Long after these moments have passed

Write more, write harder because
Practice makes perfect makes burnouts *worth it*
Write until you tip a phrase
That makes everyone go crazy
Until then
You're trapped inside this place
Door's locked and the
Entire English language sits on the other side
You're right
You're right
When you've lost the key
You just have to beat the door down
To get back inside
Use your BLUNT. FORCE. DRAMA.
COMMA
Recovery from trauma
Scream louder until it's
All we can hear
Convince us
This is finally your year

All our life, the story has
Always been the same
But this time the ending
Is going to change

For all my yelling, whispering, proclaiming, unfiltered honesty, I'm really not sure WHO I AM is coming through. I'm just a reformed piece of shit who fucked up two-too-many-times. Who never stopped laying it on the line. Who paid the price, twice, with interest compounded over time. A washed-up, fake-ass writer who's trying to convince himself he's still got a few good lines.

But there's hope for me. Underneath the disaster that all of you can see. Through all of the pain that I've caused and I've felt, I've learned how to love - *how to stand in the fire and burn, but not melt.*

This passion ignited inside my ribcage will burn until the end of my days.

I'm a walking, talking, breathing, foul-mouthed poet cliche and I don't give a metaphorical fuck what you say. I'll beat these same words repetitively into the ground until there's nothing left to say and nobody left around. My passion drips from my mouth as I spit venom at my past and speak hope into the future for something meaningful that will last. I don't deal in excuses, I find solutions and I fight for my heart, and I'll be damned if I'll let anything dull my spark. I'm probably overwhelming, I'm probably too much for everyone, and that's probably why they all probably get intimidated and cut and run.

BUT LISTEN.

I know goddamn well I'm worth the effort when push comes to shove. I love hard and I live with passion. And I never give up on the people I love.

(everything is foreshadowing)

We're all BROKE
Or
BROKEN

Trying to make the ends meet in the middle
Burning the candle on both ends
And the wax is running short
And the fire is going out

And the leftover change rattling around in my pockets
Won't cover the cost of your broken heart
I'm using duct tape for mine
Hoping it heals
Without too many obvious cracks
Without showing off the things I
Obviously lack

And maybe we're just jaded
From spending everything we have
On things that aren't worth the cost

Like *PEOPLE.*
Or like *hoping for a different ending.*

But the story seems to always be the same
And we've gotta learn, if we don't wanna burn
We've gotta stop playing the same
stupid fucking game

(BLINK)
Take a deep breath
And realize this:
Before you let it out
An entire season has passed
And everything is gone
Except
The way your hair
Stands up on your arms
When you hear that song
And the world moves on
And on
And on

It seems like nobody in this world
Knows what they want anymore
So many people, wasting their lives
Searching
But they don't know what they're looking for

It used to be
Stagnant here
Now fans push the air around
It's not quite central air
But it's better than nothing
(I guess it'll do for now)

They say
Do what you can do
The best that you can
Until you can do much better
But what if I never can?
What if this is all I am?

I know you want to love her.
Broken hearts are
So easy to fall for
But don't let yourself be the one
To protect her wounds while she heals
Remember
Band-aids are torn off and thrown away
Without a second thought

You can NOT tell me what love IS or ISN'T. You can tell me what you hope. What you dream. What you believe. But I have stared into the fire and grabbed ahold of it, and it has burned me to the bone and *I would do it again* if it means I could stand in the middle of that raging inferno one more time and feel the air on fire all around me, with a passion ignited like the sun itself, all the while knowing...the rain is coming. It's coming *inevitably* and it's going to wash this all away. No matter how bright it burns, or how much gasoline we throw on it. No matter how much kindling we scrape together to keep this flame alive. The rain is coming. And the truth that nobody tells you about life and love and passion is that even the hottest, wildest blaze eventually burns out, bludgeoned to death by the hammering, relentless downpour of the universe. We're no match for that, and so we have to learn to capture every flame-kissed moment and press it into our skin so we will never forget the way it felt. We don't have to let go. We don't have to get over it. Because sometimes holding on is the only thing that keeps us alive. And no matter how badly I've been burned, I swear to you. I swear to the universe and anyone who is willing to listen to my madness:

I will never turn down another chance to dance in the fire.

The difference between
Warming your body by the fire
And dancing in the flames
Is the difference between
Who you pretend to be
And who I am every day

Sometimes
The smell of coconut oil
Makes me question my sanity
My ability to judge someone's character
My decision making skills
And whether I am deserving of love

And other times

It just reminds me
That not everything tastes as good as it smells
Most things
Are not what you expect them to be

(Coconut oil tastes like shit)

It's an obsession
With the way things work
Or don't
With the way things
Will last forever
Or won't
Pouring over every detail
With a fine-toothed comb
Tell me
What's the difference
Between lonely
And alone
What's the difference
Between an empty house
And a happy home

We take these close up
Pictures of flowers
Zoomed in close enough
To see every imperfection
But the bee
Still pollinates
And the sun
Still shines on them
Exactly the same
And we say they're
B E A U T I F U L

And so are we.

Anyway
What the fuck is reality?
This image in my head:
Your lips, and
Your eyes locked on me
Breathing out
Pure ecstasy
This is all I can see
This is all I will ever know how to be
Putty with your hands all over me
Weak with passion
Strong when you hold me down and set me free
Swallow the truth we both know:
And then
Kiss me longer
Hold me deeper
Close your eyes and
Come with me

Can you tell the difference
Between what we say
And what we believe?
(Some days
I can barely breathe)

Can you tell me the difference
Between what's wrong
And what you think is right?
(Some days
It's not worth the fight)

Can you tell me the difference
Between healing and
Growing numb to the pain?

Some days
I think it's all the same

      e told me:
         trust your memories
They e only
Telling you what you want to see."
When I say
It's worth remembering
Just leave it at that
Don't waste your time
Romanticizing the past
Take a quick look over your shoulder
But don't stare
You're not going back.

It's
Tiny details
Like when she
Says "I love you"
First

Exhales
And falls
Into my arms
We are safe here
Together

Understanding the difference between wanting and needing and loving and cheating. When passion turns to dishonesty and gashes you open, leaving you bleeding. Leaving and seeing the truth from the outside, like the look in her eyes, when you swore to each other you were on the same page (page 12) but that book was full of lies, and now you're paralyzed, pulling the paper from the binding and the blinding truth has left you shaking as you read the words you'd underlined:

"I will live with passion until the day I die, and I'll always stay true to myself."

Just another lie you repeated. Underlined for emphasis on page 12.

I thought you were *LOVE*
In human form
The devil had never been
So clever before

Look back lightly
Remembering
Not too slightly
But rather
With purpose
When every word was poetry
When every sigh consumed me
And now I have to
Breathe
Carefully
Especially in places where there are
Ghosts in the walls
Waiting to climb inside my head

(no ghosts here)

These brick walls
Never knew your face
Or heard your voice
And so here, I'm safe
From the permeating memories
That have taken over
All of my favorite places
And it's so nice to
Breathe
Fresh air
Again
It's so calming to
Remember
Who I was before this all began

You'll never be able to
BREATHE
If you keep your head under water
You have to
Break
The
Surface

If you're having trouble
Finding which way is up
Just open your eyes
And look for the light
Kick for the surface
You've got to fucking fight

I wish I still believed
That love always wins
(But it doesn't.)

I need you to believe
That love always wins.

BUT IT DOESN'T

It's oddly
ILLUMINATING
When you realize
The only thing keeping you from
Moving on from the past
Is the patterns in your own mind
The refusal to collapse
Break down the tent
And put it away
There's nothing inside anymore
The star of the show has gone home
The stage is empty
The crowds are gone
And you're here all alone
There's nothing here worth saving
Light it all on fire
Burn it down to the ground
Let the blaze light your way
Through the rest of the night
You'll find your way home
And it'll all be alright

And you will know us
By the trail of shattered hearts
Leading right to our door.

We moved in
Made a home of this place, but
Love doesn't live here anymore.

You are the war
I am repeatedly fighting
Within myself
I won't make this mistake
Again
I'd rather admit defeat
And watch this entire thing
Collapse
Like an avalanche
Burying all these emotions
Deep inside of me

I'm reading
Stupid jokes and (tweets) about
Married life
And all the hilarity that comes with it
When I realize (again)
That it's you
It's always been you.

Or maybe it's just 3am
And I'm just lonely.
Because it's "always been"
So many people
I'm beginning to wonder
If it will ever
Just be one more

I guess I'll sleep on it.

Stop. Making. Excuses.
It's as simple as that.
Take control of your life.
Turn around now, and
DON'T EVER LOOK BACK

(And sometimes you NEED to be
A selfish asshole
Because nobody deserves to be used
And treated like they don't matter)

If you need to look anywhere
Look in the mirror
And believe in that.

Before The Beginning

The light at 5am is different
Before the world is awake
And sometimes in those moments of clarity
I realize
How much has been erased

Like it never even mattered anyway

Bottles and cans and
Give me another
So we can be okay again
And
Look at me like you care
Because it makes me forget

How I need to be apathetic in times like this and
Shove you on your way
"As long as you're happy"
And it kills me to live this way
(it's all for you)

Tattered notebooks
Full of old poems
That
Once upon a time you loved
Once upon a time
Like you and me

It's royal blue
And black inside
When you take it away
You have nothing to hide behind
And that's how I loved you
Every day and night

(When you hold me this time
I'll know it's a lie
But i'll love it the same
And pretend that you're mine)

Watching
The waves break against the wall
The most unstable stone
Protects me from this tide

I see the power and the beauty
From my seat of safety
But the water can't touch me here
And so I sit and hide

I'm safe from all my fears
But
That stone is slipping
Soon falling
And we can't hear it from here but
Destiny is calling

Soon I'll be surrounded
By everything I fear

Soon enough these waves
Will break through
And wash it all away
Soon enough these waves
Will break right through
And wash me away

This is the entire story, from beginning to
end, in such stunning simplicity that it still
manages to capture all of the complexities
and soul rushes and heart breaks and
everything in between.

This is the way I remembered that hope
has not died, I rediscovered it in your eyes,
and you almost had me believing in a
righteous god as we laughed all night.

This is how you use words to take
someone's breath away, and then stand on
their chest while they struggle for air.

This is not what we thought it would be.

This is the beginning and the end of you and me.

The notebooks with frayed edges taunt
With thoughts of things I think I used to be
And pictures of everything
That was once true about me
The words danced effortlessly from my hand
And now the sobering truth
Is that inspiration has divorced me

Line
By
Line

Chopping my thoughts off
I'll throw them onto paper or onto this screen
And I long to call it art
I long to call it anything but desperation
For the man I used to be

What have I become?
Who is this man?
Is there a bridge from there to here
That will somehow help me understand?

It turns out
I am just the same.
Again.
And it's time to start over.
But,
This time:
I have to win.

(and when I plague myself every night to do something, I always come up empty handed because of you and the way my dreams come true when I'm around you. And when I try to do what I could have done long ago, I'm only scared of everything anyways...so I crawl away for an escape. And here it comes back again, charading as someone new)

this is a story I shouldn't have to tell
and I shouldn't be here
but I'm such a pleaser

so when I say goodbye
you'll know it's your fault
(and if this keeps up)
I'll tell you how it will end

smile. kiss. fuck. me.
don't you fuck me
(everything I say has been ignored again)

I hope you love your friends
we both know this is not enough in the end
and I can say right now just how this will end.
you should know by now just why this will end.

lie. stab. end. Me.
don't you fuck me.
(I hear you, but you're not saying anything)

why do I even bother?
you know what I hate.
why do I even bother?
I fear it's too late.

"You don't know what you mean to me."
(maybe if you'd stop STABBING ME.)

No matter how many times
You let me down
And prove again and again
That you just won't give back
What I keep putting in
I can't pull myself away
There's
Something about the way your lips
Move
When you smile
When you talk
And then your voice trails off
And I get goosebumps
I swear I could watch you
And listen to your voice
For the rest of my life
But I already know
You don't feel the same about mine

Fake it til you
Fake it til you
Fake it til you
Fake it til you
Fake it til you
Fake it til you
BREAK

I took a look in the mirror
Realized I owe it to myself
To admit when I've made a mistake

Heartache - Heartbreak
Never gonna be the same
Years of pain - What's to gain
Repetition
THIS IS INSANE

Got scared - Ran away
Relegated behind the frame
All of this has been in vain
Pride wins
I won't change

Maybe someday I'll realize my mistakes
My heart is broken permanently either fucking way
Search my soul - the answer is the same
This time, *I'm to blame.*

THE ONLY FUCKING WAY
IS ALL THE FUCKING WAY

It's not too late.
It's never too late.

Cracks in the pavement
Symbolic of
Something I'm sure
If I try hard enough
There's a metaphor
Everywhere I look these days
Itching to get out
And exploit my sensitivity
Itching to
Break me down
But I still can't find
The words I need
To explain the ways you've
Changed me

please don't tell me lies
about love and forever
JUST FUCKING KISS ME

I think we mistake
passion for love. We
force ourselves to see
connections that aren't
there because it makes us
feel better, it's easier than
admitting the truth. And
then when it falls apart,
it ruins us, and we blame
each other. But really,
we do this to ourselves.

we were all hands and mouths and passionate moans
fumbling at belt buckles
in backseats and movie theaters
our spark ignited a fire
that could have set the air ablaze
burning hotter and brighter than any other
but it burned out before we even realized
and we were left naked
gasping for breath
wondering what happened

(what a fucking disappointment)

but I found myself
in the smoldering coals you left behind
and the fire burning in my heart
will put ours to shame:
a massive meteor shower
to our brief (brilliant) shooting star.

now
is not then
but then again
the difference is
never a gain

head's not cloudy
weather's clear
snow started melting
when I held you near

hear my words
and what I said
don't ignore the subtext
don't abuse the context
or nothing will make sense to you
like nothing ever made sense to me
until I held you near

listening to someone else
it's inside out
I'm somewhere else
it's funny how the rear view
changes everything
but I still just
want to hold you near

and now I know
I swear I saw you clearly
but know
I can no longer hold you near

when things implode so
suddenly, it's hard to see
where you stand in the ashes

----

nobody warned me
that the first one
who set my soul on fire
was likely to leave me in ashes

----

whatever path we take
whatever mistakes me make
when all is said and done
we'll end up right where we belong

with her touch
maybe I can hush the voices in my head
long enough
that I can pretend I forgot what you said.
but it's rough
when the promises you broke
keep repeating in my head.
what can I do to make it all fade away instead?

this is how a broken person breaks hearts.
we're not assholes
we just don't realize how fucking lost we are.

she smells of
cigarettes and cheap wine and
someone else's sex

I feel just
anxious and angry and
layers of regret

I keep getting this
Song stuck in my head
That brings me back to this
Particular memory of us
At cedar point, just past dusk
Watching Luminosity
Dancing and laughing and
In that moment
I was the absolute happiest
And most comfortable
I had ever been in my entire life

And I remember
The light in your eyes
And I remember your smile
And the way you looked at me
I knew (again)
In that moment
That I would love you
For the rest of my life

And OH MY GOD
In that moment
I almost believed there was one

If I could go back
I would stay forever there
In that moment
Of our delirious,
Heart stopping love

Every time I start to feel okay
I hear it. And it feels like a kick in the face.
"Shut up and dance with me!"
Fuck this song, and fuck this place too
And fuck every fucking reminder
Of all the fucking bullshit you put me through
But most of all

FUCK YOU.

Cold breeze
Cold beer
Cliche night
Nobody's here

These words seem to write themselves sometimes
But not tonight, and I'm not surprised
The music replaying in my head
Is like a mental block
So I try to shut it down
But it doesn't want to stop
And the stolen pen on my table
Screams to write down verses I've seen before
Repeating lines I've heard
Just changing a few words
And pretending I'm not being a whore

By now my beer is warm
And the breeze has stopped
At some point I closed the window
And now it's getting too hot
With nobody here with me
It's far too quiet
No more hands on my back
But also no more lies

So I guess now that I think of it
The good outweighs the bad
And
I think it's time for me to stop lying, too:
You were never "the best I ever had."

She said it over and over again:
"I am not them!"
But her actions spoke volumes
That her words could not defend.

You're not her?
You're right.
You're worse.

Maybe because I should have known better
But I always have to
Prove the damn universe wrong
I still miss every little moment
Even though, looking back I've realized:
It was all one-sided;
You never felt what I did
Those shared, heartfelt moments were
Pure bullshit
And I can't help how badly I'm
Destroyed by it

And waking up to this empty apartment
On Christmas Day
I remembered so many things
I always wanted to say
And the words echoes off the walls in this empty place
Where I thought we shared a new beginning
But now I feel disgraced
By these memories that just won't stop clawing
At my heart
I can't believe my life has gone on
And you no longer play a part

I can't stop playing it over and over in my head:
The day you walked away
And for some reason
Christmas day was the first thing in my brain
Well, I slept in today
Didn't have to drive across town to get breakfast
And I don't know why it ever bothered me anymore
I don't like fucking pancakes anyway

IT'S SUPPOSED TO HURT
And fucking tear you a p a r t
It's supposed to cripple you
And shatter your heart
And it's supposed to make you helpless
And willing to beg
And it's supposed to make you sometimes
Even wish you were
DEAD

And it's supposed to feel amazing
Like nothing compares
And it's supposed to make you feel
Like you're floating on air
It's supposed to piece you back together
Better than before
Because it breathes more life into you
It lets you feel MORE

If it doesn't make you feel EVERYTHING
The lows and the highs
If it doesn't make it through
ALL OF THIS
It's NOT WORTH
Your motherfucking time.

DROP IT FROM THE TOP

Are we ready?

"I don't think so."

Do you think we ever will be?

"Honestly I don't even know what that means. I only know we have to hold on tight before reality tries to smother our dreams."

I'll hold on to you, if you promise not to let go of me.

Defying definition
Casually becoming real
(Comfortable)
This is what we needed
Because
I didn't think
I was ready to feel

But maybe just a little bit
(I obviously do)

If someone's gonna
Break my heart again
      I'd like it to be you.

This is different
(Is this different?)
I was wrong before
And the time before that
So maybe I don't know
What the hell I'm talking about
But maybe
This is different
And if I'm right?
Well then dammit
We are gonna be
FUCKING UNSTOPPABLE
And baby
That changes everything

Chaotic calmness
Suddenly
Kisses Killing
Insecurity
Caress, controlling breathing
(Sigh)
Crazy, is this what I'm feeling?
(High)
Curiosity got the best of me
This is my confession, I've
Stumbled onto Someone special
Unexpected connection

Cool breeze off the lake on my face
Hand in hand with your legs draped over mine
Immortalize this moment in time:

Strawberry moon
Almost July
Look in my eyes
(Butterflies)

I don't wanna go home tonight

I'm falling hard for your beautiful
Incredible mind
You're weaving words into the strings of
My heart, binding yourself inside
Hands on skin, your lips on mine
This moment, frozen picturesque in time
Slow, steady sips from this salacious
Fountain of passionate bliss
Pure, pulsing poetry in motion, pushing
Deeper, it doesn't get better than this

Eyes locked
World rocked
Questions answered emphatically
Found my
Someone Somewhere
And (I thought)
This is exactly
Where we are meant to be

I want to kiss you
When you taste like a
Long Island Iced Tea
And we're both
Excited and a little giggly
Hands wandering
Feeling frisky
So come on over
And kiss me
I'm ready to create some
Amazing memories

You were frothing at the edges
Anxious to be devoured
And I was happy to oblige
I savored every d
                    r
                      o
                       p
Your taste still
L i n g e r s
On my tongue

A reminder of what was

Sleepy kisses and
Smiles and
Good-morning-beautiful

Meanwhile
Coffee brewing in the kitchen
(You can smell it from upstairs)
Oven warming
For biscuits
While the gravy is heating

There's no sun
Through the windows
And that's okay
I'm already in love
With you
And this quiet
Rainy
Autumn day

Come closer so I can
Breathe you in
There is
Poetry on your skin
I want to hold this love
And protect it in my heart
We will never fall apart
Never fall apart
Never fall apart

Sigh
Sigh
And release
You can breathe
You are safe here with me

I have always been perpetually
Closing my eyes and dreaming
Long for the last good thing
Or
Hoping for the next good thing
Never seeing what's in front of me

My eyes are open this time
I'm alive
And now I can see
Now I can see

I love the heat of summer
It reminds me
What it feels like *to burn*
Like my heart is exploding
Like my soul is on fire
I've always
Loved this kind of pain
No matter how it hurt me in the end
The journey is the destination
And the fire is my inspiration

Burn with me
I want you to see
How beautiful this
Immolation can be
This passion will
Never die inside me

It's 1am and we're tipsy
Let's go for a walk down Bridge Street
And we'll end up overlooking the lights
From the top of the hill
Where we can laugh and cry
And erase bad memories
One kiss at a time
One breath at a time
Let's just
Get lost
Get up
Get away
Have some faith
In something other than the inevitable collapse
We know better than that
We knew better than that

I always feel worse
When I wake up from my afternoon naps

I think the best moments in life
Are when you realize you are
Capable of making a beautiful soul
Feel beautiful things

Her smile
When you tell her
She drives you crazy
And takes your breath away

His laugh
When you're sitting at the bar
Talking all night

The way you hold and squeeze
Each other and let out that
Eyes-closed-soul-deep-sigh
Of complete, relaxed release

Yeah.
That's the shit I love.
That's the shit I live for.

There's more than just
A little mischief
Behind that cute smile
And you keep surprising me
I keep noticing I'm
Smiling to myself
Unexpectedly

I could get used to this
We seem to fit together
Seamlessly
Naturally
Comfortably
(Shut up and kiss me)

Everything about her is grace
The way she bites her lip and
Smiles to herself
The way her hair frames
The shape of her face
When the light hits her eyes
They glimmer
And there's no way to escape
The way my heart still flutters
When she looks my way
(I wouldn't want to anyway)
And the way the moves through life
With purpose and love
And a poignancy you could never fake
Everything about her inspires me
To try to be better
Every fucking day

I know, you get it
My heart is on fire
And I can't stop screaming
But maybe
I should tell you more about real feeling
Tell you something that will
Really leave you reeling
Whisper so gently that you'll
Lean
      In
         Close
AND I'LL SCREAM EVEN LOUDER
THIS IS WHAT I LOVE THE MOST

Her hand on my back
The way that smirk curls her lips
The way she sighs into my mouth
Trying to catch her breath when we kiss
Our plans for a house
With a garage and a yard
And believing that
It doesn't have to be that hard

I'll repeat these same things
A hundred thousand fucking times
Because every single day
I just want to write again and again
Over and over
How fucking happy I am
That I'm hers
And she's mine

I swear there must be a
TSUNAMI
Raging inside your heart
The way you love
Is a fucking work of art

The noodles on the stove
Are absorbing sauce
(As I say)
Your mouth is re-telling stories
In the gaps between little voices
And you said
You like my methods

Every meal I've tasted
In this new life
Is perfectly seasoned
And the air feels brisk
Like spring
Like hope
Like new beginnings
I haven't stopped laughing in weeks
You're even smiling in your sleep

And these moments
From the words we speak
To the quiet
D r i f t i n g
In between
Are everything I've ever dreamed

What's the difference between tired and uninspired?
Not much. Maybe 3 hours of sleep and a pot of coffee.
Drowning blurry morning thoughts in extra strength
caffeine for clarity while I struggle to see meaning
in...well...anything.

I spent a week at the ocean and came up empty, came
back writing the same double entendre metaphorical
"food" loving poetry that I'd been writing for months.
It's old and overdone. Maybe I'm old and overdone.
Your maybe, I'm told, is never the one. But when the
sun simmers brightly on her face and her eyes just
S H I N E, the idea that "maybe" was ever a word in
my vocabulary is...well...*dumb.*

So I'm trying to accept this version of me with less
BANG, with less brooding in the rain, and I see the
good with the bad. There's so much solace to be had in
this balance, a semblance of old tendencies lost to the
past - and that's a *damn good thing* if you asked. I'm not
necessarily writing the way I wish I could be, but my
head and my heart...well...they're finally in sync.

I just woke up
Just barely
Just a little bit but
Enough to notice you
Pulling closer
And your hands on my skin
The feeling just then:
My heart laid bare
And nothing else
Will ever fucking compare

Passion isn't always
LOUD
Sometimes it's
Quiet and
Patient and
Unassuming
Sometimes it listens
And lets you breathe
Sometimes it helps you
Pick up the pieces
And find where they belong

Passion isn't always
Screaming in your face
Sometimes it
Doesn't look like what you're used to
So it
Takes a minute to see
That it's just right
That it's worth the fight

Passion isn't always
What you expect it to be
Sometimes it's
Even better
And she's teaching me

I want to sneak booze into the water park with you and go on long drives to nowhere when we don't know what else to do. I want to make love between the sheets to our favorite songs, and in places we shouldn't be - hushed so nobody hears us. I want to race through the rain to our favorite deli where we always order the same thing from the same guy at the counter. I want to make you smile so much that you forget what it was like to ever yearn for happiness.

I want to stamp our love on the world, louder than anything anyone has ever heard - unmistakable and unquestionably BOLD.

This is the only way I know how to love and I'll be damned if I settle for anything less than earth shattering, heart stopping, life changing **LOVE.**

Every now and then
I catch myself smiling
Looking at her
Like she can save me

(Maybe she can)
(Maybe she already has)

In the mornings, I get dressed while you sleep in our bed and I pack my lunch and make my coffee, but before I walk out the door, I make my way back up the stairs and crawl back in bed next to you. Just for a minute or two, but this is my favorite part of every day.
Sleepy kisses in the dark - but I can feel you smiling
And our whispered contention:

I love you.

I love you more.

This is not a few months disguised as a temporary
forever that we know is a lie but agree to together.
This is growth and compromise and adapting and
changing as a team. The difference for us in genuinity
As in:
I genuinely believe in you and me.

We are palpable intensity like the booming thunder and the blinding lightning illuminating everything under the sky at night making it almost look like day time.

We are wide smiles and belly laughs. Jokes that make sense to nobody else. Okay. They don't even make sense to us.

We are pokes and booty pinches and smirks. Stolen kisses and hugging so long it makes us late because *we never want to let go.* Unexpected *anything,* but somehow now we expect to conquer *everything* together.

We are beautiful memories and future plans and all the quiet moments in between that I cherish more than I know how to articulate. All the words in all the languages in the world fall short of just how much this feels like *proof* that nobody else could have *ever* been enough.

Your kisses have me floating
Unexpectedly
Hands fumbling
Sighing, moaning
Quietly sexy
As I stop to find my composure
I catch that half smile
And it's over
Moving slower
Lower
Leaving you gasping
Struggling to breathe
Legs shaking
A beautiful sight to see

Breathe with me
Let me find
Inspiration
In the air between us
Let me find
Something to believe in
Where the thump
Thumps in your chest
Let us find
A path to the future
Where we travel
Hand in hand
I just want this
To be something
Actually worth all the fucking hype
I'm tired of being let down
And living a life full of
"Almost"
Every fucking time
I'm ready to be
Fucking Unstoppable
I've been ready for the universe to
Show me a sign
Give me something real
Something true
And the universe
Finally sent me *you*

Sizzle
Sizzle

Bacon grease
Pops on the stove

I forgot to buy
Half of what I need
For the breakfast I wanted to make
Eggs and salsa and bacon
Will have to do

My planning skills
Need some work
But I sure can cook just fine

Waves crash like thunder
Filling the space in between each thought
The sky over the ocean is overcast instead of blue
The sun, an afterthought, luminescing the clouds
A soft white in the otherwise gray, gray sky
I'm reaching out, grasping as each thought flies by
Like gulls through the air
Above my head, inside my mind
My toes are vanishing deeper with each
Thunderous break
As the ripples reach my feet
I'm sinking down
Into the ground
And crawling out of my skin
And all I ever wanted
Was to let you in
To invite you inside my heart, and then
Share this breathtaking view
It's so warm but it
Reminds me of the fall
And anything this beautiful
Reminds me of you

I'm only 36 years old but
So many people don't believe
In magic anymore
They're too busy keeping score
And it's a shame

It's the same words
In different context
It's the same feelings
In reverse
From the end back to the beginning
Mirroring expressions of
Everything
We remember from the fall
(They didn't know me at all)

Autumn leaves falling to me
(every time)
And this is everything we never believed
We'd be lucky enough to see

And when the sparkle
Sparkles
In your eyes
Like universal beauty at a
Universally relatable size
I know
There's still magic here

Explosively beautiful
Like a new universe is beginning
You came into my life
Like the waves crashing into the shore
Washing away the debris
Like the sunshine after the storm
Illuminating everything

I like the music our hearts make together
Looping over and over like a broken record
A connection so strong, it cannot be severed
You give me a reason to believe in forever
Worthy endeavor
Lips syncing to this tune, we will always remember
As our bodies sing a duet of pressured pleasure
A chorus of collided climaxes crescendo
Tender tempting tingling touches
Thrusting inside

SOULS SURRENDERED

Effortless efforts:
Small selfless moments
Draw the line
Breathless and defined
Stuttering lips
Whispering such small words
And fumbling hands
Doing such small deeds
This is the difference
Between those old selfish loves
And the light I see in your eyes
(One day at a time)

(Simplicity)
Your smile answers questions
I have burdened myself with
For far too many years
Easing my fears with a glance
Softening my hardened heart
With the touch of your hands

I've tasted a love like lunacy
Let it linger, delicious
And it nearly consumed me
Left me shaking, stirred, and breathless
Weak and craving more
Like an addict, antsy for the next score
But this is much more dangerous
I'll stay alive, but I've lost my soul
These glorious demons have complete control
Nothing else means anything to me

Love me like a catastrophe

I will plagiarize every word that your heart speaks to me in silence and claim this indescribable passion as art. From the very atoms that make up this dull, beating organ in my chest to your eyes and ears and soul, I want you to know that I am undeniably yours in ways that I never could have understood before this (stop-breathe-smile-realize-this-is-all-real) moment.

It sits in my chest
Like a brick of foreboding
An omen
A warning
It's impossible to shake
The clock keeps
Ticking
Anxiously
And its face waits
Same as me
But your hand on my back
Is so reassuring
That I think I can
Let myself believe

I can feel it in the way you shift your gaze
Every now and then
These cycles keep repeating
It's happening again

(Everything good always comes to an end)

I feels like
The last verse of my favorite song
Prove me wrong.
I need you to prove me wrong.

And maybe eventually
Everything's gonna fall apart
But it's not happening right now
One year
One month
One week
One day
One MOMENT can change EVERYTHING
So I'm staying right here and
I'm choosing to believe
No matter how it ends
(Or doesn't)
Fear will not control me
I will love harder
Every fucking day
Until I no longer breathe
This is the only way
I know how to be
So bring that beautiful smile over here
And just kiss me

(everything ends)

Steady
Dripping
Slipping, falling
Clipping wings
Like it's your calling
Artistic like a drawing
That feigned persistence
ALL IN
Performance worthy of applauding

and then…

Rough waters lead to stalling
No attempts at calming
World keeps revolving
I keep recalling
ALL IN

No more prolonging

You're withdrawing

And our magic is dissolving

I love hard, and when I don't get that same energy back, I never learned how to walk away. I made a commitment and I feel obligated to stay. I convince myself that if I love hard enough, I can teach her how to love me back.

I should know better by now.

This is how a good heart ends up shattered.
This is how you end up forgetting that *you matter.*

I know you won't forgive me
But you deserve to know the truth
We fucked up and I miss you

And I hope I'm still waiting for you
To choose my side
When you finally wake up and realize
That would could set the fucking world on fire

From the very beginning
We were always just
One
Long
Drawn
Out
Sad
Fucking
Ending

There is poetry
In the *catastrophic collapse*
When your heart
Can no longer withstand the pain
Because there is
SO MUCH BEAUTY
In finding the strength inside
When your heart starts to beat again

We are here to feel and to fear, to wonder and to experience, to love and hate and forgive and care and fight and fuck and hold hands and throw punches and hug it out and *question everything* and if we're lucky, find the answers with the people we love.

It's all catastrophic, beautiful, *chaotic imperfection*, and it is *utterly perfect.* For all the heartache and the pain, I appreciate the passionate, astonishing moments of joy and love even more, and I wouldn't change a fucking thing.

There's a tipping point when *always* tumbles
Becomes a walk way away
Becomes a broken promise to stay
A cracked mirror distorting everything
And my words are losing meaning

My conscious conscience is
Screaming
Of a time when all we knew was
Believing

We were:
Promises and
Always and
I don't remember anything after that, but

I fucking want it back

(It's called classical conditioning)
For my next trick
I'll make you believe in me
Long enough to mean everything
Repeatedly
Repeatedly
REPEATEDLY
Promise you that I won't leave
Repeatedly
Rpeteaedly
RPETEALDEY
Until words lose all meaning

I don't want to give away the ending but
Is there anything inside the box?
Open it from the top
Here when you're not looking
Now that you're looking, I'm not
Ring the bell
Loud enough for everyone to hear
And now you're salivating
Anticipating
Hoping and praying for
Everything I promised but

I'm no longer here
(I never was)

Tell me
What happens to the ashes
Of bonfires
After we've
Danced and laughed all night?
The next day
The wind takes them far away
And by the time anyone happens by the scene
It's like it never happened at all

Like it never mattered at all.

Burn the bridges back to that
Ghost town
Right down to the fucking ground
Demolish everything
Plant new flowers and trees
Do
Whatever you need to so
So you can *breathe*

All this time we've been taught to
Project and forget and regret
And walk away with nothing left
But I'd rather hold on too long
And hope too hard and get burned in the end
Rather than risk letting go too soon
And miss a single beautiful moment of this

It doesn't have to last forever
To last forever
We can be immortal together
If we're not together
(This love will live forever)

When we look back
I only want to see
The beauty in the way I love you
And the way you loved me

Take me back
To the afternoons on the couch
Always
Pressed for time and
Pressed against each other
Smiling and kissing and
Barely breathing

When I close my eyes
This is what I'm seeing:
That mischievous smirk
(The one nobody else pointed out)
Your hands pulling me closer
(Never wanting to let go, feeling no doubt)
Scrambling for cover under blankets
Walls crumbling
Fingers fumbling
Letting each other in
And *magic*
So much magic in the air
Between every word we breathed
And everything
That made me believe in you and me

Hiss-pop-splash
In the darkness, that familiar sound
Reminds me of the summer sun
And before the taste even hits my lips
I'm refreshed

Anticipation breaks me
As often as anything else in this world
And expectation makes me
Exactly who I am
Despite the fact that I have
Never
Lived up to anything
Or anyone

Hopes and dreams are just
A vision on the horizon
And I swear
One of these days
I'll keep every promise I've ever made
In my own way

Because I have never let go
I will never let go
Of the love in me

If you don't know how to commit and mean it and fight for what you love and listen and speak with honesty, get the fuck away from me.

I'm tired of healing everyone else's souls just for them to walk away and leave me bleeding.

When you find the one who accepts all of you and makes an effort to understand your soul you're not supposed to let them go.

But then again,
What the hell do I know?

What remains is only insignificant evidence of your *brief* fucking existence.

Memories of your brilliantly belligerent demeanor. Your tendency to stack syllables side by side into the night, never needing a sign but looking anyways, and always warning me that *someday you would say goodbye.*

I didn't listen.

I swore our souls were tangled, some type of unbreakable bond, the mind I never believed in. Imagine that - I was right all along and I think deep down I knew this was all wrong. I let myself get carried away with accepting connecting with someone who was only half there, I filled in the gaps myself with the things I swore you'd swear if you ever swore anything and I made myself believe in a you that wasn't real - so no wonder I was so surprised you would leave.

But since you've been gone, my mind keeps painting in the *brightest colors* - unfettered now, no expectations to live up to and no fear of falling down. I found my voice again and remembered how to speak my truth freely and take ownership of my identity. Truth be told, I think losing you *helped me find me.*

(This is the story of trying to squeeze something epic into a single summer, and realizing I deserve more than temporary passing passion.)

In the end
Love
Doesn't feel much like poetry
When it's left you choking
On broken promises
And you can't breathe

We ignore the truth
Right in front of our face
Because it's not
What we want to see

(We just want to believe)

Six months later
I smashed your alarm clock to pieces
In our spot in the mall parking lot
And that's the closest thing to closure
That I ever got

Make me believe in us
As I gaze into your eyes
Tell me beautiful lies
Long enough to tie me to the bedpost
And make me beg for your passion
And then walk out the door
Just like
HER
Just like
EVERYONE
Who came before

Woke up today and suddenly
All of my old love poems
Read like eulogies
They're gone but it turns out
They're not dead
They only existed inside my head

I'll spend my nights counting grief
While the sheep just laugh at me
Tellings secrets about the red flags in my
Own mirror I was just too proud to see
And I can only hope that when the day breaks
That it's not too late
For this stupid man to try again
To learn from his mistakes

Beginning to end
And every
Heart. Stopping. Moment
In between
Loving you
Has been so much more beautiful
Than I ever could have dreamed

(Thank you for ever loving me)

_ wish I could give you a better version of me
Whatever that means
Some other me who isn't splitting at the seams
Broken and unkempt
Struggling to be half the man you deserve
The man you thought you met
Making excuses instead of changes
When it's time to
Stand up
And shake it up
And push everything aside

Now instead of wishing
I'm trying
I'm trying
I'm trying

And

I'm hoping
This is the story of how our love
Only
Almost
Died

I'm hoping
We're still alive

It's usually
"Too little too late"
But maybe it's
"Better late than never"
More likely, somewhere in between
I'm trying to figure it out
But I'm not that clever
All I know is
I'm not ready to wake up from this dream

All we have for sure
Is today
And honesty
And a little bit of hope
And honestly
That's enough
To keep my heart afloat

If you're anything like me
There are certain things
You shouldn't talk about
On an empty stomach
Dry heaving is so much more
Painful
Than puking up emotions and
Flushing them away
Muscle memory
Contract
Relax
Contract
You've gotta have some substance, boy
Some sustenance
Disguised as joy
Swallow it and let it soak up all the
Alcohol
You tried to drown your sorrows with
Haven't you learned?
Memories and booze don't mix
And nostalgia is my middle name
In case we've never met
But I fucking swear
Some days it feels like
Hope is just pain
That hasn't been born yet

Reverberating
Thoughts Echoing
Cascading
These feelings
INTRUDE
Shades of
Chartreuse
GREEN with envy
Of a past that
Won't let go
Won't let you grow
Won't be thrown
Away
Until you've faced it and
GROWN

Everything about us
Has been beautiful
Right down to the way we
SHATTER
And catch each other
Gently as we can
We will rebuild
Separately, together
If we must
Two mosaics
From the wreckage of us
Twice the beauty
All the love
So different from what we pictured
But something we will be proud of
Even falling apart
We cascade
So beautifully together
We will redefine
A different kind of forever
I wish that you could stay
But in the end
I just want your heart to be okay

Excuse me but
I don't want you to be happy
With anyone else but me
And everyone can say
That means it isn't love
And I'm just speaking selfishly
And
I don't give a fuck

I want to spend
The rest of forever
Building this life
Our love
This castle
Until it pierces the fucking sky
I want our cuddles every night
And ice cream binges
And hands grasping
And deep s i g h s

I want you and me
For the rest of our lives

If you want your whole life
Following the sun around the globe
You'll never see a sunrise
You'll never see a sunset

And so

That's all I have to say on chasing love.

That's all I have to say on letting go.

Lipservice
Paid to keep the devil away
By the devil I mean
The truth about this
Life you have made

Smile through
Gritted teeth
Put on the show and
Say the things you want (them) to believe

Once upon a time
You had everything
And the world
Was trembling at your feet

This is where you're *supposed to be*
Don't try to convince me differently
Ironically
I'm better of without you
But you're not better off without me

Dripping, rhythmic
Swaying Passion
Light it up just to burn it down
Breaking hearts seems to be in fashion

Your fucking fake sincerity
Mocking my attempts at clarity
The distance between us:
Such a disparity
What happened to *meant to be?*

Connections torn asunder
Push me under
Letting you in was my greatest blunder
But that disarming
Adorable
Beautiful
Fucking
Smile
And your innocent eyes
Combined
To tear my walls down to the ground
And leave me defenseless
Against this

So now here I am once again
Struggling to turn my pain into art
I guess you were just another
Lesson learned in the war for my heart.

Made in the USA
Monee, IL
28 December 2019

19609387R00075